My Life in My Pocket
for Preschoolers
(and those who love them)

Physics and Geometry

K.L. Lewis
and
Bertram A. Lewis, Jr.,
MD, PhD, MBA, FACS

Illustrated by Megan Redlich

Waterfront Press

My Life in My Pocket

cogito · ago · contirius · sentio · scribo

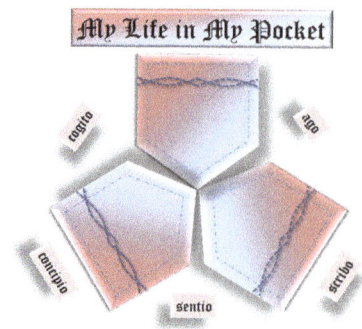

Published by Waterfront Publications
ISBN: 978-1-937504-97-7
WPP140P

Manufactured in the United States of America, Great Britain, or elsewhere, when purchased outside of North or South America

Cover illustration by Megan Redlich

Produced and distributed for
Waterfront Press by
Worthy Shorts Publisher Services BackOffice
A CustomWorthy edition

For further information contact
info@worthyshorts.com

**Everything a Preschooler
Needs to Succeed**

*Read this book and discuss the
pocket people every day and
your child's imagination
will grow every day.*

Note to Parents

When we were in college we took philosophy as required courses. We studied the teachings of Socrates as expressed in Plato's works and learned the concepts of the differing forms. Socrates had the idea that there was, "out there in space," apart from human imagination, the perfect form of any concept we humans might have. According to the philosopher, at best we communicate only a "shadow"—an imperfect version—of a form. For example, there is somewhere out there a perfect triangle, while we draw only imperfect triangles.

Socrates may have been partly wrong. Although the perfect form may not exist outside our brains, there are neurons in the inferior temporal cortex of the brain (as recognized in research of the 1980s and 1990s) that are responsible for shape recognition. There are certain neurons that fire when certain shapes are seen; these neurons (the face neuron, the mama neuron, the car neuron), interconnect to allow us ultimately to form consciousness. It is this consciousness in young minds that this book seeks to help develop.

How do we teach our children? We show them things in the world. We explain what is right and what is wrong. We help them to categorize objects and concepts. While certain neurons respond to shapes and sound, we help them to categorize what it is they see and hear. Eventually, connections are formed between these neurons.

Some might argue that the concepts discussed in this book are too advanced to teach to children younger than school age. It can be argued that the concepts we will explore are already in their minds. As Michelangelo stated, the statue is already in the marble—all we need to do is expose it! Introducing these concepts now will enable children to better integrate them when they enter school.

K. L. Lewis and
Bertram A. Lewis, Jr., MD, PhD, MBA, FACS

Live so that when your children think of fairness, caring, and integrity, they think of you.

H. Jackson Brown, Jr.
American author best known for his
inspirational book, *Life's Little Instruction Book*

Circle

A circle ◯ is perfectly round. There are no corners. There is no beginning or end.

My name is Otto and when I write my name I use a circle for the letter O.

Parent Suggestion: This is a great opportunity to point out circles in your surroundings. They are not only shapes, but patterns of motion such as the rotation of a ceiling fan. Discuss the number pi ($\pi = 3.14159$). The circumference of a circle is equal to pi multiplied by the diameter of the circle. A great demonstration of this is to wrap string around a can and cut it to circumference length. Then take a second piece of string and drape it across the top of the can and cut it to diameter length. Placing the two strings next to each other shows that the circumference will be approximately three times the diameter. Using variously sized cans, place the circumference strings next to the diameter strings to show that the ratios are always the same, no matter the size of the can.

Momentum

Momentum is the force or speed of movement.

My name is Victor and I love to create angular momentum as I swing back and forth.

Parent Suggestion: Explain to your child that force is needed to start the movement of a swing. That's why they have to be pushed; the resultant swinging is momentum. Tell them that when they are swinging, the swing's movement draws arcs or partial circles in the air.

Square

A square ☐ is a shape that has four corners and four sides. Each side must be the same length as any of the other sides.

My name is Shelly and I love to search for squares in the constellations of the stars.

Parent Suggestion: Talk about how squares are part of our everyday lives such as square dancing or the playground games 2-square or 4-square. Point out the various square shapes you see around you like a picture frame or a calendar.

Triangle

A triangle △ is a shape with three sides and three points. Its size can vary, but all sides must touch at each point.

There are three types:

△ equilateral △ isosceles △ scalene

My name is Tony and I love to play the triangle in my school band.

Parent Suggestion: Point out the various triangles around you; less apparent than other shapes, finding them can be fun. Explain that the straight lines are the sides of a triangle and each corner is called a vertex.

Rectangle

A rectangle ☐ is a four-sided shape in which all the corners have the same shape. The sides across from each other are always the same length.

My name is Remington and I love to read stories on my rectangle-shaped computer tablet.

Parent suggestion: Talk about different things in the world that are shaped like a rectangle—an ice cream sandwich, a box of cereal, their bed, a juice box, and, even a huge football field. To increase your child's thinking capacity, try to think of more rectangle-shaped items each time you read this book. Draw pictures of rectangles to demonstrate that the line lengths can vary from rectangle to rectangle, but it is still a rectangle.

Polygon

A polygon is a shape with three or more straight sides. The angles are not necessarily the same among all polygons, but all the sides touch at the corners. Some examples of polygons are:

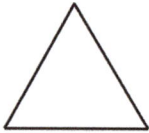 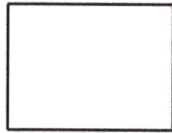 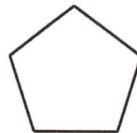 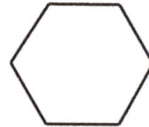 

Triangle	Quadrilateral	Pentagon	Hexagon	Octagon
3-sided polygon	4-sided polygon	5-sided polygon	6-sided polygon	8-sided polygon

My name is Bertram and I like all the shapes that the painter Pablo Picasso uses in his paintings.

Parent Suggestion: Do a computer search for Pablo Picasso's paintings and point out the various polygons. Spend time each day discussing art and how being creative is a wonderful way for them to express their thoughts and feelings and how this helps to advance civilization. Teach your child the importance of continuing to improve their minds and how this will help them to make their dreams come true.

Pentagon

A pentagon is a shape that has five sides and five corners. It is also a polygon because it is a closed plane figure with three or more straight sides.

My name is Paige and I love to paint pentagons with my paintbrush.

Parent Suggestion: A pentagon is a shape found on soccer balls. Talk about the Pentagon being the name and the shape of a government building—that the people who work there seek to keep the United States safe. You may wish to use this subject to discuss our government and how we have a president who is part of the three branches of government: judicial, legislative, and executive.

Hexagon

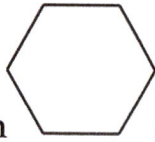

A hexagon is a shape with six sides and six corners.

My name is Hillary and I love to use a magnifying glass to look at the hexagons in the honeycombs of a beehive.

Parent Suggestion: Explain that bees build honeycombs which they fill with the nectar of flowers that they bring to the hive which then becomes honey. Discuss how bees are marvelous architects. Point out their role in pollination, without which plants could not reproduce and provide us food.

Point

A point .   · is a very very small dot.

My name is Nathan and I love to search the sky for the points of the constellations.

Parent Suggestion: Explain that a constellation is a collection of stars that traces an imagined shape and how each star represents a point in that shape. Explain to your child that there are billions and billions of collections of stars in the sky (called galaxies) and billions and billions of stars in each galaxy—and that we are actually made of stardust. How cool is that?

Line

A line ╱ is a single, long stroke (that can be represented by a mark) that has no thickness and extends in both directions without ending.

My name is Marvin and I love to draw an X-Y axis on the whiteboard.

Parent Suggestion: Tell your child that an x-axis or a y-axis is part of the notation of geometry, a kind of mathematics that pertains to shapes. Ask them to look for shapes in the room. Describe how the TV or the bed is shaped like a rectangle, or the base of a lamp can be round, like a circle. Explain how geometry enables one to measure these shapes and that they will learn how to measure shapes in middle and high school.

A line, although a simple concept of geometry, can allow the discussion of many other concepts such as dimensionality. You can demonstrate the concept of a graph and how it quickly illustrates numbers visually.

A line is a one-dimensional object. Discuss how we live in a three-dimensional world and point out that length, width, and depth are the measures of an object.

Discuss the concept of infinity and how a line in geometry does not end.

Lines

Lines are straight marks on a page. If the lines cross, they are intersecting lines. If the lines never cross, they are parallel. If the lines cross like the letter "t," they are perpendicular.

My name is Xavier and I love to write my name using intersecting lines to make the letter X.

Parent suggestion: Point out to your child that parallel lines move in the same direction and never cross each other and that intersecting lines cross each other and can create the letter X. Demonstrate on paper how parallel lines do not cross. Here is an example of parallel lines:

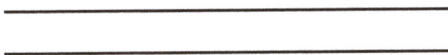

—————————————————

—————————————————

Sphere

A sphere is a three-dimensional object like a ball.

My name is Jamie and I love it when my mommy slices oranges to make circles.

Parent Suggestion: Although an orange is not a perfect sphere, it is a quite good representation. Cut an orange in half to show how the cut surface is round like a circle then measure the distance from the core to the peel at a few points around its circumference. Each measurement should be the same.

Cube

A cube is a three-dimensional shape having six equal squares as its sides.

My name is Kat and I love to see how high I can stack blocks.

Parent Suggestion: See how high your child can stack such things as books, blocks, apples, and so forth. Practicing to stack things improves their fine motor skills. Count the surfaces (sides) of a block to show that there are six and each is a square.

Time

Time is a way to keep track of the movement of the earth around the sun.

I am Earth and it takes me one year to travel all the way around the sun.

Parent Suggestion: Point out how your child's age represents the number of times the earth has traveled around the sun; that each birthday is one circle around. If they are three years old, the earth has traveled around the sun three times in their lifetime. Point out how the earth has circled the sun more times because you are older.

Space

Space is where everything happens.

My name is Quincy and I love to look at space through my telescope. I can see many planets and I can see our moon, which is the earth's satellite.

Parent Suggestion: Discuss how all things exists in space—like, people, cars, your pet dog, and big objects like the planets and stars.

Gravity

Gravity is a force that pulls everything toward the center of the earth.

My name is Gladstone and I love to jump really high because gravity always brings me back down to the Earth.

Parent Suggestion: Discuss how we cannot see gravity, but we feel it. Gravity is what makes things fall when we drop them. Try dropping various items of a variety of weights to see whether they hit the floor at the same time.

Speed

Speed means moving fast.

My name is Lydia and I love to solve math problems with great speed.

$0+1=1$
$1+1=2$
$2+1=3$
$3+1=4$

Parent Suggestion: Help your child to remember basic mathematical operations like one and one is . . . . Point out that once they remember these facts they will be able to call upon them with speed. Set a timer for sixty seconds and count how many addition problems your child can answer in a minute. Establish a daily schedule for doing this and similar mathematical manipulations.

Direction

Direction is the act of moving from one place to another along a straight line.

My name is Greyson and I love to go hiking and use a compass to help me to determine direction.

Parent Suggestion: Describe the various meanings of direction—how, when you request that your children pick up their toys, you are giving them direction; and how, when you drive your car, ride the bus, or walk, that you are moving in a specific direction.

Mass

Mass is those parts of a thing that resist movement.

My name is Bethany and my backpack is heavy because it is filled with books, paper, and pencils that create mass.

Parent Suggestion: Discuss how everything on earth has mass. First, talk about how a rock has mass, as does a glass of water. Point out how (in general) molecules and atoms make up matter and how the more atoms there are, the more mass an object has.

Weight

Weight is heaviness.

My name is David and some of these grocery bags are too heavy for me to carry from the car, but I try anyway because I always want to help.

Parent Suggestion: Discuss how different things weigh different amounts—and how weight has different meanings. For example, talk about how our heart can feel heavy when we feel sad, and how our heart can feel light when we feel happy. Discuss how weight is different from mass. For example, the weight of an object on the moon is one-sixth of what it is on earth. While an object will have the same number and the same kind of atoms (have the same mass), it has a different weight on another planetary body because of the force of gravity being less on a smaller body. The mass of the Moon and the greater mass of the Earth, each creates a gravitational field. In a sense, weight can be seen as the result of mutual attraction between the Earth or the Moon and an object.

Temperature

Temperature is a measure of warmth or coldness.

My name is Ursula and I love to play soccer in the fall because the weather is just right.

Parent Suggestion: Discuss how temperature can be measured. Describe how your body responds to the outside temperature. Explain how temperature will tell you when you are sick because your internal temperature has risen above 98.6 degrees.

Electricity

Electricity is the flow of electrons (found inside atoms) from a region of higher energy or voltage to a region of lower energy or voltage. This is called an electric current.

My name is Carl and I charge my electric car by plugging it into the outlet in the garage.

Parent Suggestion: Discuss how electric cars are better for the environment and that electric current moves because of magnetic fields.

Sound

Sound is the vibration of matter.

My name is Frank and I love to play the drums that create the sound my eardrums hear.

Parent Suggestion: Discuss how sound is everywhere and a part of everything we do and is even in things we can't see, like the sound of the wind.

Light

Light is something that makes things visible.

My name is Shirley and I love the light from the sun that shines through my bedroom window every morning.

Parent Suggestions: Discuss how, even when it's cloudy outside, the sun produces light and how nothing moves faster than light. Sunlight takes about eight minutes to reach earth.

Energy

Energy is a lot of activity.

My name is Zelda and I use a lot of energy as I skate around the rink. My energy comes from eating healthy food.

Parent Suggestion: Discuss how healthy food gives us energy and how it is important to sleep well so we have energy to do the things we love to do.

Kathy Lynn Lewis, a Johns Hopkins University graduate, is a leading expert on Self-Advocacy. She has devoted the last seventeen years to helping families with children with special needs to advocate for their children. She travels around the country speaking and leading seminars that help individuals and businesses achieve success through goal-setting and outlining "what they want to have," "what they want to be," and "what they want to do." She is the CEO of *My Life in My Pocket,* a company that helps students, businesses, and individuals realize their potential by understanding what Earl Nightingale states: "We become what we THINK about," and that the impossible takes a little longer, ***but not much.*** Ms. Lewis is the author of the *My Life in My Pocket* book series (www.MyLifeinMyPocket.com). She lives with her husband and two daughters in Tampa, Florida.

Bertram A. Lewis, Jr. MD, PhD, MBA, FACS, is the Chief of Surgery at Florida Hospital Zephyrhills. He is a practicing urologist with a Bachelors, Masters and PhD in Biomedical Engineering from Johns Hopkins University; his MBA is from St. Leo University. He lives in Tampa, Florida with his wife and two daughters. Bertram and Kathy have been married for over twenty-three years.

www.ingramcontent.com/pod-product-compliance
Lightning Source LLC
Chambersburg PA
CBHW061413090426
42741CB00023B/3495